Ayasha and the Jingle Dance

by Christine Kohler

Ayasha looked in the mirror, admiring the jingle dress her grandmother had sewed for her. It had beautiful metal cones, formed from the lids of tin cans, which jingled when Ayasha danced. She couldn't wait to wear her jingle dress the next day at the pow-wow. The Native American ceremony was having a jingle-dance contest.

Gently, and with great care and pride, Ayasha picked up her Ojibwe feather fan, and held it in her hand. She had always admired the fan, which had been handed down to her by her great-grandmother. Ayasha moved her feet in a zigzag pattern, first in one direction and then the other. She closed her eyes, lifted her arms, and fluttered the fan.

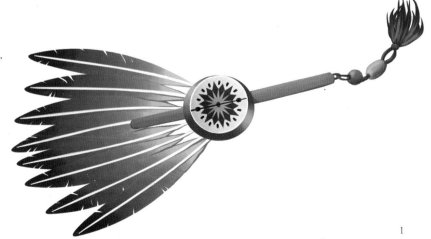

Just then, Ayasha's dad drove into the driveway. Ayasha set the fan on a chair in the hallway and hurried to show him the dress. When she opened the door, a puff of air blew the feather fan upward. *Whoosh!* Ayasha didn't notice that it floated high on top of a cabinet.

The next afternoon, Ayasha put on her jingle dress and checked that she had everything she needed. But where was her fan?

Ayasha's dress tinkled as she rushed into the hallway, but the fan wasn't on the chair. Ayasha looked underneath it, but the fan wasn't there, either. She buried her face in her hands.

Ayasha felt a hand on her shoulder. "What's wrong?" Grandma asked.

"My fan has disappeared," Ayasha cried. "What will I do? I can't get another Ojibwe feather fan now."

"Take a deep breath and tell me everything you were doing right before it disappeared," Grandma said.

Ayasha closed her eyes, lifted her arms, and pretended to flutter the fan. Grandmother followed her movements with her eyes.

"There's the fan!" Grandma announced, pointing upward.

Ayasha opened her eyes and gasped. "How did it get on top of the cabinet?"

Grandma chuckled and said, "Isn't it feathers that make a bird fly?" Grandmother reached up and handed Ayasha the fan.

Ayasha hugged Grandma and said, "Let's go to the pow-wow. I'll be the happiest jingle dancer in the contest!"